THE AMERICAN POETRY REVIEW,

The Honickman Foundation is dedicate_____ ____te spiritual growth and creativity, education, and social change. At the heart of the mission of the Honickman Foundation is the belief that creativity enriches contemporary society because the arts are powerful tools for enlightenment, equity, and empowerment, and must be encouraged to effect social change as well as personal growth. A current focus is on the power of photography and poetry to reflect and interpret reality, and hence, to illuminate all that is true.

The annual American Poetry Review/Honickman First Book Prize offers publication of a book of poems, a $3,000 award, and distribution by Copper Canyon Press through Consortium. Each year a distinguished poet is chosen to judge the prize and write an introduction to the winning book. The purpose of the prize is to encourage excellence in poetry and to provide a wide readership for a deserving first book of poems. *Great Exodus, Great Wall, Great Party* is the twenty-third book in the series.

WINNERS OF THE AMERICAN POETRY REVIEW/
HONICKMAN FIRST BOOK PRIZE

1998	Joshua Beckman, *Things Are Happening*
1999	Dana Levin, *In the Surgical Theatre*
2000	Anne Marie Macari, *Ivory Cradle*
2001	Ed Pavlić, *Paraph of Bone & Other Kinds of Blue*
2002	Kathleen Ossip, *The Search Engine*
2003	James McCorkle, *Evidences*
2004	Kevin Ducey, *Rhinoceros*
2005	Geoff Bouvier, *Living Room*
2006	David Roderick, *Blue Colonial*
2007	Gregory Pardlo, *Totem*
2008	Matthew Dickman, *All-American Poem*
2009	Laura McKee, *Uttermost Paradise Place*
2010	Melissa Stein, *Rough Honey*
2011	Nathaniel Perry, *Nine Acres*
2012	Tomás Q. Morín, *A Larger Country*
2013	Maria Hummel, *House & Fire*
2014	Katherine Bode-Lang, *The Reformation*
2015	Alicia Jo Rabins, *Divinity School*
2016	Heather Tone, *Likenesses*
2017	Tyree Daye, *River Hymns*
2018	Jacob Saenz, *Throwing the Crown*
2019	Taneum Bambrick, *Vantage*

GREAT EXODUS, GREAT WALL, GREAT PARTY

CHESSY NORMILE

The American Poetry Review
Philadelphia

For my sister and my brother
and for Michael Adams

Cover art by Nora Normile
Book design and composition: Gopa & Ted2, Inc.
Distribution by Copper Canyon Press/Consortium

ISBN 978-0-9860938-1-4 (cloth, alk. paper)
ISBN 978-0-9860938-2-1 (pbk., alk. paper)

9 8 7 6 5 4 3 2 1
FIRST EDITION

Contents

INTRODUCTION

CHOOSING "Great Exodus, Great Wall, Great Party," I single out for attention a mind that is not only smart, curious, and original, but one that I feel is genuinely daemonized, "touched," and authentically weird. I choose a voice that is heartbroken, vulnerable, enraged, tender, and hilarious. I choose a work borne of an imagination that is unpredictable, fearless, probing, self-questioning, and marked by the influence of a hidden wisdom that some might consider folly. For instance, I find it brilliant that in a poem inspired by The Book of Tobit the poet identifies herself with Leviathan as opposed to the human agent of divinity in the Biblical story. By doing so, the poem magnetizes to itself several interesting ideas about the sacrificial role of the poet as *pharmakos*.

The same poem suggests that one of the most powerful goods derived from consuming poetry is to cure blindness and distinguish lust from love, a notion worth pondering for days. Meanwhile, reading a group of poems in which color and the awareness of color figure so strongly, one wonders just how conscious the poet was about the etymology and connotations of the word *Phoenix* when it appears as a place name in a poem about omens, birds, blood, and regeneration. When that word appears, the entire poem becomes dyed by it. These poems are full of ideas zipping by, ricocheting off each other, and fueled by a desire to know, to understand. The speaker wants out. Her sentences and lines search for an Archimedean point beyond the inadequate accounts of the world she's inherited. The speaker wants in. Deeper in. To the heart of the matter. I have no idea if the author of these poems consciously invented their speaker, or if the poems are actually the confessions of a psyche completely exposed to something like the creative unconscious. The subject of the majority of these poems is synchronous experience, otherwise known as acausal ordered-ness, which would account for their fidelity to their moment of composition and their drive not toward non-meaning, but meanings beyond the precincts of mentality and its calculations. And since the logic by which these poems proceed is the logic of acausal ordered-ness, I think it's important that these poems be read out loud to oneself if they are to surrender their complexities and depths. Otherwise, their quick and subtle modulations of tone and their vivid enactment of their subject matter might be missed. In fact, while reading this book, I kept wondering if language itself isn't altogether a synchronous experience par excellence, words being both material and non-material instances of time, voice, body, mind, concept, thing, mark, symbol, and world. Of course, that was when I wasn't thinking, "These poems are ridiculously funny. So why am I so heartbroken reading them?" Thinking, "These poems are so sad. So why am I laughing?" My sincere hope and wish is that this author not only stays weird, but that she continues to deepen toward her famously weird and prophesying sisters, and then grows beyond them to sit in the very lap of Hecate.

Li-Young Lee
January, 2020

EVER

All the books on time
are pretty good.

When the boat carrying bubonic plague was approaching
the Sicilian harbor of Messina everyone on shore said,

"Wait . . . look,
something's wrong with that boat,
it's moving too slowly and only
a few oars hit the water at a time."

They watched it come towards them.

When the boat arrived
they saw how everyone
was either dead or dying.

There's an essay I'm purposefully not going to cite
because I think t.s. eliot gets enough attention
that says the books we read now change
the books that were written before them.
They actually *change* them.

This is time inconstant.

There are different types of time:

Earth time

Sacred time

Another type concerned with human behavior,
for instance, collecting figs, erecting columns, returning goats

Tropical time

Star time

Atomic time

Dream time, supposedly,
and a type of time
that undoes itself,

lets me read the book that Amy wrote—
which deals primarily with elephant grief—
and then read "The Wasteland"
to find it populated with the deaths of elephants
who I had not realized in high school were there.

Alternatively,
if you don't believe me,
try this:

Read a letter I wrote you five years ago.
Read it now.
Read it after reading
each subsequent letter I sent,
in particular the ones
where I admit,

"I have loved you
quietly
from across the wall."

Terrible Music

I misunderstood what kind of boat party we'd been invited to.

You were screaming in your sleep beside me,
thrashing like a dead shark
held in the arms of a living man.

You were both the shark and the man, which impressed me.
My dreams don't scare me like that anymore.

Sweating, you woke
and walked swiftly off the deck.

Time passed until, over salmon,
I got to congratulate us
on our perceived humanity.

Agreeing heartily, you poured
champagne into a flute and I was like,
He just ruined that flute.

You proceeded to play the most terrible music.

Love hath made me stupid.

I should've thought,
This guy is a terrible musician, shut it down,
but instead I became
a shallow bowl of strawberry milk
riding a fictional boat through a very real storm.

Anyway, after the terrible concert and the great sex it was morning
and in the kitchen you noticed a paper bag folded in on itself,
a spoon cracked with white yogurt lying on top.

Because of my knack for espionage
what you didn't notice was me,
seated in the corner like a chair.

I watched you find the spoon,
break it apart from the table,
and lift it up to the light.

You stood still, gentle as a rock
sinking to the bottom of a lake, and I thought,
When we die, may that someone lift us purposefully as that.
May they consider us a little then decide
we are suited to our death before they let us go.

HYMN FOR DAN

We went to visit our brother.

They had a special, blue room
for the purpose of waiting.
A counselor came over and
called my sweater, "too provocative."

Nora started laughing
and then I started laughing
and then our brother came out
and told us about the squirrel he had been feeding
packets of peanut butter each day to pass the time
and how the squirrel was now too fat to climb trees
and he was worried because winter was coming
and we were all laughing and crying from the laughing.

We stayed as long as we were allowed
then Nora and I walked
back through the snow,
towards the hotel
five years ago.

Last night, in bed, I typed
Being and Nothingness
into a Wikipedia search.

It was a book my dad had put
in the basement bathroom
of the house we grew up in.

Something else about my dad was on Sundays
he put a cabbage leaf on my head
in an effort to calm me down.

Let me draw you a diagram
of that perfect, tranquil hat.

Being and Nothingness is a book
about phenomenological ontology.

Now you don't have to read it,
you're welcome.

When I was fourteen
I read *The Stranger*
and it spoke to me until
"I fired four shots more into the inert body."
Really put me off.

But, at sixteen, I met a girl named Tania
and Tania loved Camus. So I tried again
and read *The Fall*. But *No*, I decided,
closing the book, *I'm not an existentialist,*
I'm just sad.

Tania and I continued our friendship despite this.
One evening, we sat on the floor of my bedroom,
tattooing our feet with India ink. I was working hard
on a crescent moon when I looked up and saw that Tania
was almost at the end of the phrase *Russian Fatalist.*

I remember how Tania's parents lived far away
and sent her care packages full of cigarettes.
I remember that she dressed up as a Q-tip for halloween
when the rest of her friends dressed up as nurses.

And I remember what it felt like
when the moon on my foot disappeared.

This wasn't meant to be a hymn to all that.

Do you know what I can't write about?
My brother.

Hymn for You

May you find coins.
May you unlock things, e.g., mythic eggs.
May you destroy the coins.
May I take your coat.
May the dice throw their combinations at night.
May it be June then July.
May it be that you are fourteen in July.
May water rise.
May it have to do with the moon.
May you have sex somewhere special.
May this pinecone fit in your car.
May G*d grant you this.

Last Day

Marie says it's shattering to be recognized.

For what you want
to reach back towards you,
say, *I see you.*

Maybe this is why
I'm crying all the time again—
in the chip aisle at the grocery store,
at my beige, wipeable desk,
in bed, six AM, suddenly awake
like a big leaf
flipped over in the wind.

My eyes are turned
to liquid and suspended—
not pouring out the sockets,
just warbling on the edge of themselves,
like screen savers.

Blue, white, silver, pink, black.
To name five of the colors involved.

I turn the volume up and watch
little gray parentheses ripple out
from the cartoon speaker icon.

))))))))))))))))))))))

Oh g/d, oh g/d, oh g/d

I am 1,000 times more shattered
than I have ever been before
barring like ten other times.

I feel invisible. Or no,
what I mean is
I can't see me.

But you can
if you want to.

Just stand across the street.

I figured that out last night
walking home from church.

My bedroom lights were on
and in the window there stood Sam,
swaying in his small, white underwear.

He was smoking a joint and
changing the radio station.

He had a baseball cap on.
It was deeply moving.

So there it is, I whispered.

Matt Cook has a poem about death
where he says it's like seeing
your own house from across the street.

Was this the reverse of that?
Or that?

MORTAL

A fly shakes its life off into my coffee.

Do you know the old saying,
If you're on fire,
put that fire out?

Taking care of a man is easier
than having a man take care of you.

I'm scattering
lettuce around the bathroom
like a vegetarian maid.

Understand
a column of silvering
light for what it is:

the moon selecting
one animal for you to notice.

Last night I had a line
from the TV guide
stuck in my head:
sexy slippery cum sluts.

Hours later I lay beside you
in a dark room that belonged to neither of us.

You were falling asleep
when I turned on my side to whisper,
"And the silken, sad, uncertain rustling of each purple curtain
Thrilled me—filled me with fantastic terrors never felt before;
So that now, to still the beating of my heart, I stood repeating,
'sexy slippery cum sluts.'"

Are we grateful or are we complicated?
I can see a mountain from where I'm seated
but keep forgetting to feel a large enough amount of awe.

Ok, there, I feel it.

WITNESS

Washing my hands rapidly with nowhere to be, I splash some
milky white water on my stomach. It drips in three rivulets onto
the elastic band of my underwear and I realize how sexless my life
has become. I run a hand under the faucet, wipe the soap off
my skin. I feel depressed. Mine is the loneliest bathroom on earth.
People are like, *ha ha your poems are funny*, and that's a kind of a
miracle. I'm grateful. It's nice to share the joke of my existence
with you. But, like the fish who tried to swallow Tobias' foot in a
lesser known moment in the Bible, I seem to function one way,
when my life is really hidden in another.

It's not the food of me— immediate, salty, eaten by the river—
that you need. It is my weird gray organs: my heart, gal bladder,
and whatever that other one is.

Tobias didn't know about the heart— that it could be burnt
when he sought to bed a haunted beloved; that it could drive
The Destroyer from the room, for the both of them— nor did he
know of the gall bladder, which, if made into an ointment,
could cure his father's blindness; cast a film over his eyes
that he might peel gently back.

I think I'm devastated. I don't know if Tobias was.
Probably not, because he wasn't cursed, and I am.

For seven years, I have stood at this sink
and sometimes, though rarely, I forget why.

This is a momentary kind of a thing.

//

THIS

I ask Joan for help with all this.

This is your life, she says.

Classic.

FIELD

The sky is full of lightning
and the sound is coming in.

You're alone, pulling weeds
up from the ground.

There is micah in the roots:
gold glitter clinging to the thread—

it's terrifying to realize
anything all at once,

as the first drop of rain to touch you
makes you realize it is raining.

And Send a Bird

I ignore omens all the time.

A bird in each airport terminal,
pale fruit split open in the grass,
a man bearing his low
center of gravity
just outside my house
talking loudly on the phone about seeds...

Someone even says "Augury" on the bus
as I ride to meet you. Nobody says augury.

But I don't quit my job
when the lights go out
the same moment as you say "tomorrow"
and I wake from dreams
of fire overtaking the town, but still
I light the stove for coffee.

In Greece, everyone said "augury"
and everyone watched as a snake,
the precise color of blood
pouring out of a bag at night,
swallowed nine baby sparrows
and then their mother.

And what I'm saying is everybody really reacted!
They set sail for Troy! And then stayed there! For ten years!

They left their wives, their favorite and least favorite
children, their soft and fallow fields, their vineyards
ripe with fat purple grapes, their beds and custom
fire pits, all because a snake
killed ten birds nine years ago.

I watch a small, brown bird
trying each window at the airport.
She is trapped and I am afraid
will die here. But I get on my plane anyway.

The layover is in Phoenix.

As if that weren't enough,
in this terminal again
appears a small, brown bird
charging towards the windows.

How is it
that I can ignore all this
and board a second plane?

In the ninth year, actually, the Achaeans forgot why
they'd agreed to spend so much time away from home
and asked to leave. But an auger everybody trusted
was there to remind them. Is that right?

I guess it doesn't really matter.

This poem is more-so about how
an identification with snake behavior/ bird murder
cost a lot of people their lives.

Driving me home from the gym
Thom notices the moon.

"Hey," he says "that big upside-down moon
is the same as the one on my arm."
and holds it up to show me.

"An omen," I say with authority from the passenger seat.

He asks what type.

The music on the radio
is from twelve months ago.

"It's a good omen, I think,
to drive towards something
you have on your body."

I shift around in the dark
as Thom changes the station.

"Years ago," he says,
"around the time when I began to lose it,
I saw omens everywhere
and followed all of them."

A train makes the customary sounds
and I wonder if I have been insensitive
by bringing omens up so casually.

I really love Thom
and want him to know
that in Ancient Greece nobody
would've thought he was crazy.

You Have Been Happening

I'm fine, things are fine. You know how space
can crack into three, like the light inside
your eyelids? Yeah, me too, I know about it.
Today, though, the dark searches me like a wound.

I am here in the window, I'm lifting my foot,
beneath me is soil and above that white wood.
Last night at O'Connell's I split into two,
the room was a river I had to swim through.

Be here. Right now. Be here.

I found ten things to show you:
a blue bird pulsing in his skin,
a wet car in the rain combed over by the wind,
my body like a stone dropped deep into my sheets,
the roses grown inside of walls, how the wild patternless repeats.

If you were here, I'd name them for you—rock and self and cliff—
but when I see you, I'll pretend I didn't carry you through this.

Moon Captured

Earth complete
First bacterial life
Photosynthesis
Meta bacteria
Free Oxygen
Sexual Reproduction

Sounds pretty good.
All of this though, mind you,
is interspersed with ice ages
followed by what's called the
Worst Ice Ages,
which includes but isn't limited to
Algae Death.

Then comes the Visible Life Era,
which, p.s., we're still in
according to the way people treat me.

Plants ashore
Insects ashore
The Frasnian Catastrophe,
which we can gloss over,
wasn't his fault,

Trees and seeds
Vertebrates go ashore
Early reptiles
are now clomping around Pangea
then there's another catastrophe
in the Permian Terminal,
which is like a train station for lizards

where nothing changes, nothing moves
but guess what it makes way for

Modern amphibians
Dinosaurs, very famous,
then another catastrophe,
this keeps happening, before

Early mammals
Birds
Modern flowers
Modern placental animals
Early horses
Bats, rodents, and early whales,
which is sort of an amazing moment,
scale-wise,

but wait
hold on,
I know what you're thinking:

that this list will continue
in some supposed order

but what if I tell you
that after early horses
and early whales,
comes the monk

who in quote-on-quote 1198 AD
wrote the following sentence in his diary
on the subject of a fire that woke him up
in the middle of the night:
The young men among us ran,
some to the well and some to the clock

And what if, after the monk,
came the death of Mary

and only after that
a surge in new mammals
the invention of eyeglasses in Italy
the domestication of dogs
my semi-religious outdoor wake
the big bang
the murder of Archimedes,
bent over, drawing circles in the sand,
and any repercussions for his killer?

Or, what if, *before* all this,
sponge divers discovered
the rusted antikythera mechanism
at the bottom of the ocean

surrounded as it was
by the dark metal limbs
and heads of men?

Look around.

There's a guy down here
whose flute broke off
and now he's blowing nothing.
We have that in common.

But I digress.

The point is
maybe pottery
preceded a period
of ten million years of cold—
all the cups and bowls and plates

were captured in the ice
and when they thawed
dolphins swallowed them
and went absolutely extinct.

I'm not saying these are facts,
I am just saying "what if."

In the grocery store, I see a bird again.

Everywhere I go inside these days: birds.
And outside, too, but that's not so remarkable.

150 million years ago all this bird stuff began.

Lemuel said twenty years ago
a Scotch tape plant exploded
and there remains in that place
a field of static electricity so strong
that if you walk within 12 blocks of it
you get sucked straight in.

That the flies
all hang in mid-air,
like stickers.

Maybe I've got that wrong.
Maybe I've lost your trust,
as a historian.

Huts and fishing
Woolly mammoths
Warm interlude
Sheep and clay tokens
Pictograph writing
The wheel

Biblical flooding
Regular flooding
Monotheistic sun worship
Sharp cooling
Jewish religion begins
The Iliad
Goths
Rome falls
Bubonic Plague
Easter Island settled
Very warm climate
Black death
Joan of Arc
Little ice age

I don't know how to get it back.
Because truthfully,
I don't believe in time.

My death began
ticking away inside me
the moment I was born.

We contain
all kinds of things,
all types of ice,
and the grass,
it grows backwards
soon as you shut the door.

COLOR THEORY

It's getting so purple in here it's breaking my heart.

On the Eve of St. Agnes, your stalker wears big lilac mittens and
rearranges your fruit.

A girl can't sleep alone.

I keep expecting the moon to wax.

There's a flat violet color that I learned in church.

*I'M ENGAGED. I'M THE COLOR OF MY BONES. SPACE IS
DEFINED BY BIRDS AT DIFFERENT HEIGHTS.*

The sky goes green.

Then slate then storm then ice then bells then pebble.

Some other facts: a lemon is blue inside, when you cut a green apple
open it's purple inside and flat as a wet metal, blue raspberries
have pink seeds, a pink storm fills with black lightning.

Am I afraid of the dark?

The life inside a dark blue egg?

A curtain lifts to reveal the same thing behind it— that I'm an old
pond with a fire in it.

There was a time when I could only focus my eyes on the smallest
thing.

At a certain point, it's all too much, so you think about your
laundry, what to make for lunch, briefly your rape, then
an expanse of black velvet.

How a darkness spread over their eyes.

Green makes it go violet.

Blue makes it go yellow.

Yellow makes me believe in the color blue.

Going Home

Today I am sad.
Even in the beautiful shower
where the soap is large and amber.

Fact

Did you know that up until this year
I thought Prog Rock was Prague Rock
and I was like, *Good for Prague,*
people really seem to love their music.
But then again, only people I hate.

Hi Nora

Remember how we had a beer with those priests at Lowlands
and when we left they said "Be seeing you"
and they meant in the afterlife?

FEEDBACK

We don't get a lot of opportunities to give men feedback.
Personally, I hated being raped.

Devotion

I'm heading into impossible topics
like the 52-hertz whale or Spring.

GOVERNESS

"Govern this!" I cried
opening the net bag of bananas
and beginning to hurl them from the car.

My Hobbies

To meet you underwater.
To faint inside a lake.
To spit into a bowl.
To cry into your spit.
To piss upon the dirt.
To love you like this.

There Was a Forest of Pines I Loved for Years

Marie says *Remember,*
you're writing these poems for god.

I'm about to ask her what type of poems god likes when the wind
    picks up, sending a flood of small, round leaves down the street.

Got it, I say.

This isn't supposed to be the same poem again,
though many of the same things will happen in it:

I *am* reading a book and I *am* transformed
(even if only in the little way Nora and I used to joke about,
holding the door open saying, *This door just changed my life*)
when it says, "There was a forest of pines I loved for years."

I ask to borrow Adam's car
and drive to the nearest forest.

The light fades to navy blue,
settling at its darkest up ahead.

This place is full of briars
and wet stars and I am
in the thick of it, little pricks
in my shins lightly bleeding
as I walk out and out . . .

Okay, is this the garden
of forgiveness? Is this
the depth of being??

Am I writing the poem
I need to write to survive???

Make the wind come back—
I'm listening!
I'm wet and it's dark
and I'm listening.

///

MOTH

"doobiedoobiedoo"
would be a nice thing
to hear someone
with a cool voice
say right now.
Maybe a bug
with a tiny microphone.

Last night I thought the moth on my carpet
was dead, but I investigated the scene gently
and found out the moth was alive, which was
great. I got to carry her outside on my finger
and feel like "hey look you're helping!"

We stood on the back porch
not wanting to climb off. It felt
like our blood was merging.

I am a gentle girl, mostly.

Can people change? Like,
"I'll stop now"? I think yes

because an example is I stopped
being afraid of white eastern european men
who are over 6 feet tall b/c I knew it was just b/c
one white eastern european man who was over
6 feet tall happened to beat me up one night

and it gave me
sort of a stupid
animal reaction
for a while,
but like I said

I worked through it and it's
totally chill now I'm past it.

There is a moth on my bed.

Hello, there.

Very familiar and
suddenly obviously
alive.

It feels good to watch
her fly around— land
there, land next to me.

Even if she lands on my face,
I'm cool with it. I accept.

I am a column of loving you.

I'VE NEVER SEEN A TREE

I'm reading a book on consciousness
that tells me I have never seen a tree
when August calls to tell me
there's a supermoon outside.

I leave the library to find it,
but the buildings are tall and surround me
and I'm not even 5′8″, I just tell people that.

This is frustrating
until two girls
run towards each other,
each yelling
the other's name
'til they collide.

Oh, there it is: full and yellow
against the waterblue sky,
light in the way
the sky sometimes gets at night,
with dark, misty clouds
floating past and around it.

I love the moon and I love girls,
but my book would say
I've never seen the moon and
I've never seen a girl,

I have only seen this planet's moon
and these two girls and in my mind
have formed their concept.

The book says language
asks us to understand
the concept as the thing itself,

that the pear tree I steal from
on my walk to church becomes
one part of my belief in trees.

I ride the bus home and pass Le Rouge, as always,
a lingerie and costumes store on the side of the highway
that I can't for the life of me figure out how to enter.

J says the moon is always
the same size in the sky,
that you can measure it with your finger.

It just appears closer or farther away from
the things we've built and believe in.

You live in "New York,"
which feels far away
because I live in "Texas"
in a low, yellow duplex
with a torn, purple hammock.

It seems there is some secret to unlock
in the language of our distance
that could transport me directly to you...

If I could look ahead of me
and not call this space
would it collapse?

When I get off the bus
the sun is setting.

I can't believe I've never seen a sunset.

Misunderstood

I wrote a joke on the bathroom mirror in toothpaste.
It was about how there were four combs on the sink,
which I think is a remarkably high number of combs.

Who were you brushing?? I wrote
and drew a fictional animal with long hair.

My roommates came home and it was like christmas for me,
very proud of myself, lying in wait under the covers, listening.

I heard the mean one, Simon, tell his girlfriend,
There's a snide note in there
about too much hair in the sink,
which was an incorrect reading of my joke.

This caused in me a panic so acute I fainted.

Luckily I was in bed already,
so this was not so different from falling asleep,
except for one potentially noteworthy difference,

which was I dreamt all night
that the men who've attacked me in this life (and will ever later)
were swimming through dark, thick water
towards my sleeping body.

I couldn't move because my body was asleep and
I couldn't hide because my body was glowing,
like a white ember/ridge of maggot/sliver of soap.

I could not turn
the damned light off!

The water glowed 'round me where I touched it.

Because of the glowing
I saw it was red,
thought, *maybe this is not water...*
thought, *THIS IS BLOOD I AM SWIMMING IN,*
and remembered

the time I drove to Washington, DC
with a girl named Carly who liked to lucid dream
and how in the car Carly told me she had met a shaman once
and that that shaman told her,

In a nightmare, Carly, if you are being chased,
turn around and walk right back towards the thing that is chasing
    you.
Only one of three things can happen: it will disappear,
it will change into something else, or you will wake up.

When I woke up
I was staring in the mirror,
looking at myself
through the toothpaste message.

Who were you brushing?? the mirror asked.

I reached out and began to smudge *brushing??*
until all it said was *Who were you*

DISSOLVER

The rain is so crazy.
It reshapes my face.

Meanwhile, Marie
tells me about Peter.

How Jesus knew
he would betray him.

How he warned him, even.

For seventy-five days, I have
been walking and swallowing.

Peter said, *I won't do it*,
but then, of course,
I say that all the time.

And all the time I try to see it:

the symmetry breaking,
the sun going down,
the grass, the dirt, the sand, the night,
any of it, I'd take any of it—

show me
just one thing
in its wholeness.

No, don't.

Masculinity and the Couple Things
I Know about It

Lying in the grass at Barton Springs, I decide to tell Sam and Lucas
that testament comes from the root testes. *Because,* I say, *men
used to make agreements by gripping one another's inner thigh.*

Wow, they say.

I don't really know these boys yet. I just arrived like 5 minutes ago.

Yeah, I go on. *And if a woman's husband was brawling
and she tried to intervene by grabbing his opponent's testicles*
(which, I might note, it has never occurred to me to do)
then her hand had to be cut off. For she had violated

the sacred space.

I remove my glasses like, *Howdya like THAT?*

They walk me down to the water. Inside, I inhale
more of it than I mean to and can't stop coughing.

I paddle, behave wobbly.
We arrive at a rock.

Check out the new testament, says Sam, inclining
his head towards an older man's half-erection,
buoyed up in its thin, black thong.

Behind him, a bachelorette party kicks into high gear.
I am not lying, it's just true, it's just the facts.

3-feet-tall, pink, inflatable peni are born from their bags.
The bride-to-be, in a fluffy white veil, lofts hers on high.
Her seven friends scream, *Yes! Ok! Diane!*

It's like I cast a spell with my fresh, biblical anecdote.

We get out of the water
but the water
does not get out of us.

Back in the grass it pools around me:
my water penis.
My brave, handless life.

Some Thoughts

I pull a pink book off the sill,
it's cold and my favorite—
The Land Where Other People Live—
and read it in a tent of blue sheets,
the cold coming through
where the fabrics too thin.
I haven't been writing I haven't been
opening the mail I have been burying
lizards in the yard, picking pink nonpareils
out of the furniture to make a poem
you can lift a letter out of, like
"egret meteor shower"
now think about the letter "e"
think about standing naked
in a shower full of men you don't know
a shy and holy space
with eight faucets and the sky
breaking out beyond the glass,
light cut of a meteor
scraping the sound out your bones,
this is the page I save
for all the poems I'm embarrassed about,
this room's the room I save
like salt and ice to return to,
freaky in my death suit / freaky in my fat hat.
I passed Nora a joint while she was FaceTiming somebody.
Yee Gods! Am I a volatile person? No!
Joan and Liz and Nora,
you know me better than I know myself
know me better than I know myself—
am I the world's worst absolute worst
animal? What is going on why can't I
crack open and just be better already?
I want to be so much better so much kinder

so much stronger so much smarter so much
calmer so much less self-involved
oh and I want to be the kind of pretty
that makes people use it as a qualifier.
Like, "You know Chessy, you met her last fall,
she has glasses, she's really pretty?"
And they'd be like "Of course, Chessy,
the girl from the fall who's so pretty."
When of course, I know what they say...
"You know Chessy, you met her last fall,
she slapped that guy then choked on some ice?"
Ay Carumba, am I right?
And YES sure I could spell that right SURE,
but that's not why we're here sheeple!!!
We're here to make a mess of things
and we are GOOD
very good professionals! Ya duh!
Genuinely though,
all you fuckers with your sex lives
and your central air and your Hamlet...
hkgvbjop ;dbfjdkdzfn tmetuds
I'm supposed to see this new therapist tomorrow
but what I want *instead* is to park my car
in the driveway of a strangers house
and flash my lights 'til they come out
to hear the music I wrote them.
This is the music I wrote them.
Man.
Really wish I hadn't told this woman why I needed to see her when
    we spoke on the phone . . .
For Gods Sakes.
For Gods Sakes off 5th Avenue.

In the End

I believe in believing.
It's done well by me.

So when Death arrives in bedsheets
like a child in the yard I inhale,
perform a miracle where I turn
bread into toast, and seek to ready my soul.

Every last thing, everybody arrives and I have
three, seemingly revelatory thoughts:

> We think the heart is the mind
> and then we think the mind is the mind.

> Sometimes, in a sexy mood, I'll say, *destroy me.*
> Mostly though, tbqh, I've been like, *wait, no, don't.*

> We wait, ah, whether we know it
> or not, for a day like this: a last one.

Satisfied, the child floats towards me
in the narrowing and relative grass.
My vision pares down to a point.
It reminds me of something.

I remember that I am a goat. No, that's not it—
it's the toaster. I remember to unplug it from the wall.

Proud of myself, I lean through the door,
a motion I expect to feel silky & ethereal,
but which in fact translates to my tripping
over Nothing and tumbling out into the grass.

I look up at the ghost, in what is now
a vanishing thimble of sight.

She is pulling her sheet off in one long, fluid tug.
The yard turns to static before she is finished,
but I feel positive that,
>   had I been able to see it,
>   she would've had a face.

////

Deep

I came to this café to do some soul searching.

One of my big fears is humor
getting in the way of my becoming
what I would like to call now an emotional genius.

So I am going to get real tonight.
I'll start with the world.

Here's the world:
No, here's a dog:

black and brown,
relatively petite,
contains a map.

The map is detailed
and red and illuminating,

but you can't get to it
because this is a complicated dog
with a largely uncomplicated mission

who won't open up until he's underground,
much in the mortal tradition.

BY MYSELF

I took a pretty intense bath in the woods.
I stood up
and the water rushed out of my body,
my eyes, vagina, nose,
I'm kidding, it was normal, it was a normal bath.

I am doing a lot of research here, though.

It is all for the horror film I'm making
about finding peace.

Submerged in bathwater—
when you stop exhaling furiously through your nose
for fear of how horizontal you are—
there is a lot to hear.

This is scary and familiar.

This is the soundtrack for my film.

In the morning,
walking out barefoot in my underwear to get the mail,
I feel I am walking towards myself
and take note of it,
like, for character research.

When the main character is alone
she is walking towards herself
and she knows exactly where she is.

So I guess she is both the protagonist, you know,
and also the killer,
sort of stalking herself all week,
keeping internal tabs on accident.

Like, the more in touch she gets with herself
the more danger she is in
because she knows her own whereabouts
and can't really hide at all.

Some of the footage I have taken includes:

barn shots,

a couple interviews I conducted with myself,

and then just

whole minutes of black—

empty ink—

but for a little red light
appearing and disappearing,
attached to a black dogs neck.

Maybe that is all a horror movie is:

When a girl does not want to be a caretaker anymore...
How she is realizing who she is when she's alone...

That something turns on inside her
when the dog walks into the bushes
and its light goes out.

That for a moment she finds herself
hoping it won't turn back on.

THE FIRST MATTER

A lot of men in the books I read
are supposedly still alive.
I wonder if they're still afraid.

Right now, in the school library,
holding my place in a book
on The Secret Art of Alchemy,
nobody's raping me. Superb!

The book says if you achieved
THE TRIPLE CROWN OF ENLIGHTENMENT
then you were inducted into
THE BROTHERHOOD OF LIGHT,
which means you are still alive today.

Maybe you're in this library with Ally and me.
Maybe you're standing outside it. Either way,
you're experiencing your crown. Do I hate you?

The most divine secrets
were never written down.

For instance, the Druids were,
I'm pretty sure, wizards,
and this alchemical stuff's the same—
we used to keep what was precious private.

That's how it ought to be:
that our secrets light us up,
that we spit the rest out.

_____

_____

_____

Soon!
Someday, so soon,
I will do it.

I'll say your name out loud.

FEELING IT

Crowded rock mountains/
clear wet rivers going white.

Lemuel points to beaver dams I can't see.
But I trust him.
He is trying to help a small bug
fly out of our moving Saturn.

When I was born well who knows.

My favorite song plays.
It makes me cry.
May that it play forever.

I'm feeling the kind of happiness
you try to hold onto—
so lit and soft
it's almost sadness.

Put Lonesome Crowded West on again.

THE ENVIRONMENT

This morning I read *Earth First!* in the kitchen
and it gave me a lot of new ideas and perspectives
even though I'm admittedly speciest
and what Thom calls anarcho-skeptic.

I'm I, but sometimes
I'm you, and mostly you

sit still,
gather together
some material
possessions in a box
and say, *Belongings,*
under your breath.

What else is under your breath?
I wish I was under your breath.

My mom wrote me a note,
signed it from her and my dad:
You are so proud of you.

I hope she meant *We.*

The real thing is nothing.

It's that either a bug bit my eyelid just now
or I have a stye because of my issues and stress.

I shook nine clementines out of their pink, net bag this morning,
like, *oh g/d, oh no, oh lord,*
when I realized one had atrophied and turned green.

I rinsed the remaining eight in the sink,
desperate to protect them.
I need to protect these clementines
from the passage of time.

From outer space
you can see
what we've done here:
the tailings ponds,
the long walls,
it's all in the magazine.

We act alone when we witness ourselves,
but we aren't.

Now I see it,
under my breath.
Now I don't.

You have been living and aging.
You are so proud of you.

LIKE POEM

Andy makes it sound
like he had a crazy hairstyle when he was my age,
but I saw a picture it was not that crazy.
I say I want to cut my hair off when I quit my job
and he says, *I'm going to hold you to that*.

Stop trying to press me into things.
Stop lying about your hair, Andy.

I got FaceTimed awake this morning,
naked, and it was kind of romantic.
I had fallen asleep the night before thinking:

when worse
comes to worst
in pain
and worst says
all right, come in.

Something special
is that even though it took a little while
my parents really came around to me.

Can you tell me again about babies
and how they assess reality
by taking it into their mouths?

How nothing exists until they taste it?

I want to build a careful nest around your name.
I want to pull a splinter out of your heel
and feel it coming up in my spine.

Even now I can feel it.

Maybe this will be the summer I stop thinking altogether.

I pack my mouth with dirt and pretend
I have been buried alive.
My arms are pinned to my sides, but still
I am going to figure out how to hold you.

The Boom of Nothing

If you only have one trick,
it had better be a good one.

But don't take my word for it,
consider the porcupine,
the horseshoe crab, eyelids.

My family joins me on the bench.

I mean this legally,
we're a family of jurors.

I powder my wig.

My sister's like, *stop
that is not your wig
that is my hair let go.*

Vulnerable Man

At night, when we're not looking,
small blue flowers
close their mouths
in the grass.

Rainbow

Yes,
you know about this natural phenomenon
and what it does to the heart.

Like candies and toys
in a glass cabinet at the arcade:
it breaks it.

The sun catches
inside four glass bulbs
in a long string of previously
unlightable lights.

My neighbor screams when she sees this.

It was once common to scream
when a lightbulb lit up,
but it's pretty rare now,
so congratulations to her
on what is generally considered
an antiquated reaction to light.

I want one more week on earth, at least, I think.

But it's no matter.

I know the great miracles
are the ones I don't think to request.

And anyway how devastating
to get what we ask for—
a dolphin key chain,
more beautiful than an actual dolphin,
suddenly extracted, yours.

/////

TRANSFER

~
###

This is how my life begins.

Temporarily, you'll forget
why I brought us here—
haphazardly and into the past.

I will try often to remind you.

Leah says we each contain
a magnet. Dalton drops
an alka-seltzer tablet into his water.

I'm 1,000 years old.

Leah is lost
and keeps me
on the phone.

My magnet's broken, she says,
pausing, I imagine, at a cross-road
or else some dark, unfamiliar tree.

When I was younger,
everybody was.

Three women at the bakery
actively encourage each other.

Do it, they say.
Do whatever you want.

Dalton drinks his living water
with thin fingers. We stopped,

walking over here,
at a magnolia tree
he knew about.

It was small and zesty
so we laughed at it

before remembering to be humble
and bending ourselves over
to prove we believed.

The perfume released
some blood in me.

In the bakery bathroom I found my
baby blue underwear burned bright red.

All kinds of
transformations
calm me:

vaginal bleeding,
seasonal stuff,
Dalton and his water,
Leah and her magnets,
the evolution
of modern cartography,
even this chair—
how it materialized

as I pulled it out
from under the table.

How it darkened, but kept
what I understand to be
6 PM inside it.

Ok, Look

I went into the woods alone alone
and came out wet and aware
of the blight that's killing the aspens.

You could write things down just as they are,
just as you see them. You could try that.

My Life So Far

I enjoy talking to the man beyond the wall.
His pants are like one bad triangle.
At home, he can see the statue of liberty
just by sitting on his stoop. I live by the water, too,
in my own way, meaning by its code.

When I was fifteen I was new
at my high school and a girl named Dawn
gave an impromptu presentation on water.

No one asked her to and she made the poster
in under ten minutes. *We do not pay enough attention*
to this element, she said to the room. I thought she was crazy,
but I listened. Now, I heard, she does a pretty good deal of ecstasy
and hula-hoops in small but elaborate outfits on the west coast.

I asked my co-worker if he felt he had gotten to know the statue
     of liberty,
watching her from his home like that. I said, *have you noticed that*
     she's walking?
and regretted it immediately. Why am I always challenging
     people?
In the article I'd been reading at my desk the author asked, out of
     nowhere,
is this the hill you want to die on? and I didn't know. I don't know
     what hill this is.

Last March I got beat up at night and it wasn't anything like I'd
     always pictured it in my head.
I just crumpled to the ground and blurred as his boot swung in
     and out of my face.

All my life I had trusted in this buried power
that would reveal itself when the time came.

I used to keep my backpack on
at the parties my brother would take me to
in various basements around Pelham, New York.
My mother called it *skating around the edges.*

I think I grew up this year. Does saying that negate it?

Do you have to let go of everything to grow up?
How about just most of it?

~~A group of boys gathered around me in the woods.~~

~~*Let me light that for you.*~~
~~It seemed normal at first, and then the questions.~~
~~*Is that too big? Does it hurt?*~~
~~I didn't understand why~~
~~they were talking about my cigarette like that~~
~~until I looked up at the boy who'd fucked me~~
~~while I cried the night before and saw him laughing.~~

~~His friends had formed a circle around me. They were quoting me.~~
~~*It hurts*, I had said to him. And the next day, they all said it back.~~

~~My greatest fantasy has been the same thing for seven years.~~

If I could have any one thing
it would be the chance to go back
just this once to kill them.

This is not the hill I want to die on, but I am willing to.

When I realized the statue of liberty was walking
my whole life literally came into focus.
Do you know what that feels like?

When your face opens up on the sidewalk and you realize
you might die, but still you are not powerless? For instance,
maybe in the spot you die a poisonous mushroom could grow
and the man who killed you could eat that mushroom.

Never mind.
What matters is that I am
will be ready next time.

I am not skating around the edges anymore, et cetera.

I thought this poem might be funny. I forgot what My Life So Far
    has been.
But it has been funny. And if it wasn't midnight I would tell you
    in what ways.

Notes

"Ever" refers to Amy Lawless' book *My Dead* and T.S. Eliot's essay "Tradition and the Individual Talent"

"Hymn for Dan" quotes a line from Albert Camus' *The Stranger*

"Last Day" refers to a poem by Matt Cook called "My Wife's Car"; this poem is for Sam Dusing

"Mortal" quotes Edgar Allen Poe's "The Raven"

"Witness" is based on The Book of Tobit

"And Send a Bird" is line 310, Book 24 of Caroline Alexander's translation of *The Iliad*

"Moon Captured" is for Michael Adams

"Color Theory" was written inside James Turrell's skyspace "The Color Inside"; it references some of the weird shit Porphyro did in John Keats' poem "The Eve of St. Agnes"

"There was a forest of pines I loved for years" is line 88, Book IX of Robert Fitzgerald's translation of *The Aeneid*; this poem is for Marie Howe

"I've Never Seen a Tree" references Julian Jaynes' book *The Origin of Consciousness in the Breakdown of the Bicameral Mind*

"Some Thoughts" references Audre Lorde's book *The Land Where Other People Live*; this poem is for Joan Ziminsky, Liz Carr, and Nora Normile

"The First Matter" refers to the book *Alchemy: The Secret Art* by Stanislas Klossowski de Rola

"The Boom of Nothing" is for Leah Wellbaum

"Rainbow" is for Thom May

Acknowledgments

When I showed Thom my first draft of these acknowledgments he said it sounded like I was dying. Fair enough. I had, in fact, tried to individually thank everyone in my life as if this was my last chance to ever tell them how I feel. So, instead, I want to just say thank you— to all of my friends and teachers and family—for everything.

As for this book "in particular," I would like to express my gratitude to:

The Michener Center for Writers and each of my teachers and peers there

Hedgie Choi, Jackson Holbert, Sarah Matthes, and Michael Adams for their edits and attention to this book

My family, for, like I said, everything, haha: Mom, Dad, Dan, Nora, Nat, Sam, Leah, Marie, Joan, Liz, and Thom

The Honickman Foundation, Copper Canyon, The American Poetry Review, and Elizabeth Scanlon in particular, for your guidance and support

The Grind and The Core

The journals in which some of these poems first appeared: "By Myself" in *fogmachine.life*, "My Life So Far," "Terrible Music," and "Moon Captured" in *jubilat*, "Ever" in *Academy of American Poets*, "Hymn for You" in *Narrative*, "Hymn for Dan," "Field," "There was a forest of pines I loved for years," "Color Theory," and "And Send a Bird" in *The American Poetry Review*

And finally, Li-Young Lee, for selecting this book. If your introduction had just said, "I read this," I would've been like, "Well, this is it, we've arrived, put a fork in me, I'm cooked." I am so grateful— in this world and the other nine.